Meet my Neighbor

Meet my neighbor, the librarian

Marc Crabtree

Author and Photographer

🌳 Crabtree Publishing Company

www.crabtreebooks.com

🌳 Crabtree Publishing Company

Meet my neighbor, the librarian

Dedicated by Michelle Lal:
For my parents Manohar & Sushma Lal and my sisters Sonia & Ruby Lal.

Author and photographer
Marc Crabtree

Editorial director
Kathy Middleton

Editor
Reagan Miller

Proofreader
Crystal Sikkens

Design and prepress technician
Samantha Crabtree

Production coordinator
Margaret Amy Salter

Print coordinator
Katherine Berti

Photographs
All photographs by Marc Crabtree except:
Shutterstock: pages 3, 24

Library and Archives Canada Cataloguing in Publication

Crabtree, Marc
    Meet my neighbor, the librarian / Marc Crabtree.

(Meet my neighbor)
Issued also in electronic formats.
ISBN 978-0-7787-4559-4 (bound).--ISBN 978-0-7787-4564-8 (pbk.)

    1. Lal, Michelle--Juvenile literature. 2. Librarians--Canada--
Biography--Juvenile literature. 3. Library science--Juvenile
literature. I. Title. II. Series: Crabtree, Marc. Meet my neighbor.

Z720.L235C73 2012   j020.92   C2011-907921-6

Library of Congress Cataloging-in-Publication Data

CIP available at Library of Congress

Crabtree Publishing Company

www.crabtreebooks.com   1-800-387-7650

Printed in Canada/012012/MA20111130

Published in Canada
Crabtree Publishing
616 Welland Ave.
St. Catharines, Ontario
L2M 5V6

Published in the United States
Crabtree Publishing
PMB 59051
350 Fifth Avenue, 59th Floor
New York, New York 10118

Published in the United Kingdom
Crabtree Publishing
Maritime House
Basin Road North, Hove
BN41 1WR

Published in Australia
Crabtree Publishing
3 Charles Street
Coburg North
VIC 3058

Contents

Meet my Neighbor

Meet my neighbors, Michelle Lal, and her parents, Sushma and Manohar. Michelle is a librarian.

Michelle works at a **library**. A library is a place where books and other forms of information are kept. It is a place to learn and have fun.

Michelle does many different jobs at the library. She is reading a story to this group of children and their parents.

Librarians also help people find information. Michelle is teaching this woman how to use a **computer**.

Michelle helps the woman search the internet for the information she needs.

Michelle uses a computer to find out if the book this woman wants is in the library.

Michelle also teaches children how to find books in the library. She is helping these children with their reading.

This man wants to find books about cars for his daughter. Michelle shows him where to find the books he is looking for.

People can borrow books from the library and bring them home.

Michelle uses a computer to keep track of who has each book. She tells people when they must return the books to the library.

These children are excited to bring their books home.

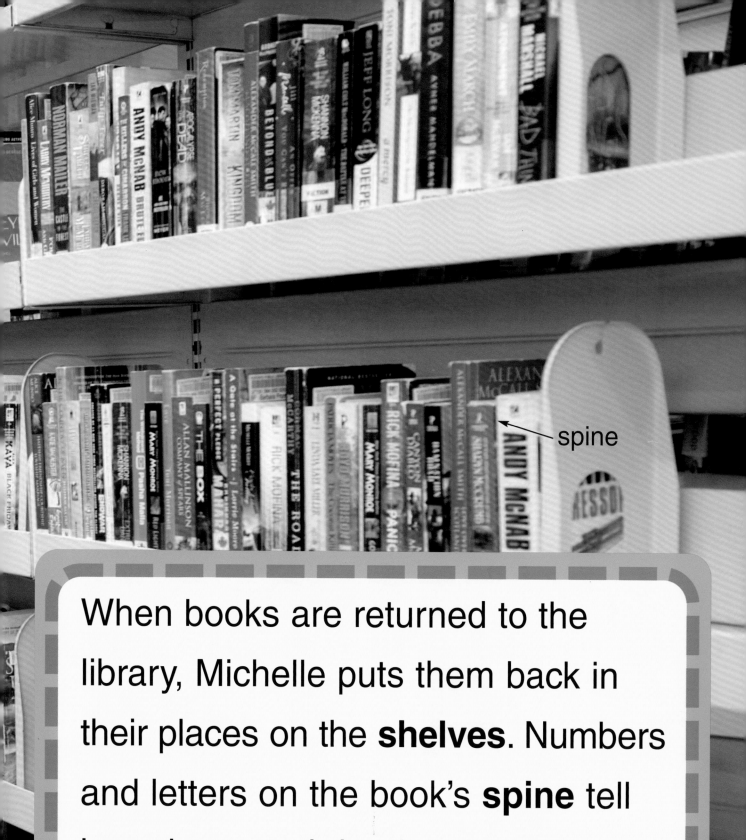

spine

When books are returned to the library, Michelle puts them back in their places on the **shelves**. Numbers and letters on the book's **spine** tell her where each book belongs.

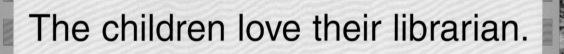

The children love their librarian.

Today, Michelle is excited as she heads home from the library. Tomorrow will be a special day for her.

It is Michelle's wedding day! Her family is Indian, and she is wearing a wedding dress from India.

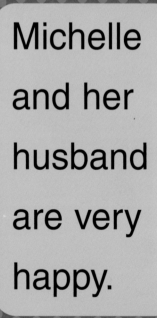

Michelle and her husband are very happy.

Glossary

computer

library

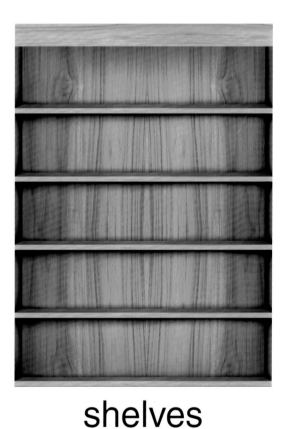
shelves

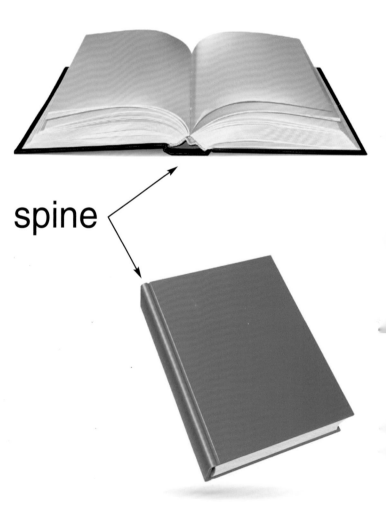
spine